Saving the Earth

by Megan Litwin

PEARSON
Scott
Foresman

DK

What You Already Know

Land, water, and air are important to us. The surface of Earth is made up of land and water. Some kinds of land are plains, hills, and cliffs. Some kinds of water are rivers, lakes, and oceans. There is more water than land on the Earth's surface.

Rocks and soil come from the Earth. Rocks are nonliving things. Rocks are a natural resource. Living things can use them. Soil is a natural resource. Soil has sand, clay, and humus in it. Sometimes the land changes over time. Water and ice can make rocks break and change. This is weathering. Erosion is when wind or water moves rocks and soil.

People use land, water, and air in many ways. Land is used to grow trees and food. Minerals come from the land. They are found in rocks. Water can be used for bathing, drinking, and cleaning. It can be a home for animals. Living things use air to breathe and grow.

Some natural resources could run out. We can help save land, water, and air if we reuse, reduce, and recycle. This book will help you find ways to reuse, reduce, and recycle to help save the Earth.

The Earth

People use natural resources from the Earth. We need them to live. But we have to take care of the Earth. We can help save the Earth's land, water, and air. We can help if we do the three Rs.

The three Rs are reduce, reuse, and recycle. We reduce when we use less. We make less trash when we use less. We save resources.

We reuse when we use things again. Things can do the same job more than once. Things can also be changed to do new jobs.

We recycle when we make old things into new things. Old car tires can be recycled. They can be made into mats for floors.

The Earth's resources are important to us. It is our job to care for them.

We need to work together to protect the Earth.

Reduce!

Did you know that most people in the United States throw away over two pounds of garbage every day? That is as much as a small dog weighs! You can throw away less. Think about what goes in your garbage cans at home and at school.

Find ways to throw away less.

Turn off lights.

You can reduce the resources you use. Turn off lights after you use them. This can save electricity. Do not forget to turn off water taps when you are done. Running water can waste many full glasses. Try turning off the water when you brush your teeth too.

Turn off faucets.

**Take buses
to save gas.**

Take the school bus or walk if you can.
This will save gas. One bus can carry as
many people as about twenty cars!

Carry your lunch in a lunch
box. Use it again and again.
You do not have to throw
away bags each time.

Use a lunch box.

Reuse!

Use things over again. Use them in the same way. Use them for something different. You can use a basket or a pack for your groceries instead of lots of bags. Save the bags you do use. Reuse them for your next trip to the store.

Shopping bag

Brown bag

There are many more things you can reuse. How about giving your clothes to other people when they get too small for you? That is a great way to reuse! Pass clothing on to small children. Give clothes you do not want to a store that can sell them to others.

Clothing can be used again.

Use both sides of a piece of paper.

Use both sides when you use paper. This will reduce how many pieces you need. You can reuse lots of things for art. Paper rolls, plastic bottles, old containers, paper bags, and pieces of gift paper can all be turned into beautiful art.

What can you use again for art projects?

Recycle!

Lots of what we throw away can be recycled. Recycling turns trash into something we can use. It helps save resources. Recycling paper saves lots of trees. It also reduces how much trash there is. Look for the recycling symbol on things you buy.

Recycling symbols

Many everyday things can be recycled.

There are many things that can be recycled. Paper, glass, plastic, and metal can all be made into new things. Many places have special recycling containers. In some places, people come to pick up things in these containers. In other places, people bring things to a recycling center.

Special containers help us recycle.

Things from nature are easy to recycle. Old leaves and grass can be put in a compost pile. Old food can go in too. Compost becomes fertilizer. Fertilizer can be put on soil to help plants grow.

Compost

Work Together

There are many ways you can help save Earth's resources. Reduce, reuse, and recycle. You can do your part to help. Put recycling containers in your home or at school. Remember the three Rs. We can all work together to help protect the Earth.

Glossary

compost   a mixture of leaves, grass, and other things used to fertilize soil

containers   things used to hold other things

fertilizer   something that is put on soil to help plants grow

recycle   to make old things into new things

reduce   to use less

reuse   to use again

trash   something to throw away